# MASTER YOUR SELF THERAPY: How to Gain Self-Awareness, Grow and Understand Your Emotions

By

## Dr. Broonie R. Moore

# Table of Contents

# Chapter One

## Self-awareness and Better Self-Knowledge

Many individuals lack the self-awareness necessary to respond to the following inquiries: When nobody else is around, who are you? What situations make your skin crawl and where do you feel most at ease? Do you understand why this is so? Do you comprehend who you are and why you behave the way you do?

Sometimes we don't need a deep explanation for why we behave in a certain manner. But a thorough grasp of who we are is essential for pleasure. Stress may be reduced to the greatest extent feasible when we are aware of who we are. We may set limits once we are aware of our triggers. We may choose pleasure and surround ourselves with nutritious relationships when we have self-knowledge.

Happiness depends on our ability to understand ourselves. It's time to quit going along with the herd and doing what everyone else does. Find out how you might better understand yourself by reading on.

Do you know who you are?
Give the following questions some consideration.

What are your advantages and disadvantages?
Describe the ideal day for you.
Who would be your ideal dinner companions?
What causes you to smile?
What frightens you?

You likely have a solid understanding of who you are if you can respond to these questions without difficulty. If you are having trouble, you may need to be a bit more self-aware and observant while you go about your daily activities. Being a social species, humans find it challenging.

We look for security and safety in a group from an early age. We often adopt the traits of a group to fit in. Our dietary decisions or immunization practices may have a big influence on this.

Do you like the music you're listening to and the clothing you're wearing, or are they just there to make you fit in? Is the vehicle you're driving approved by others? Are you reading this book only to stay in touch with your pals, or are you enjoying it?

Are your views your own or are they the product of other people's influence? Knowing whether we are behaving in our true selves or for the sake of our peers is a crucial step towards self-awareness.

The advantages of knowing oneself
A lot of advantages enter our lives as we have a greater awareness of ourselves. This includes a higher sense of pride and self-esteem.

Additionally, knowing ourselves enables us to be more compassionate toward ourselves. We are gentler to ourselves and base our selections on how well we know our preferences and areas of interest.
It is extremely easy. Our self-confidence grows as our grasp of ourselves does.

Five techniques to improve self-awareness
I've been searching for a deeper relationship with myself for the last several years. To fulfill my desire for self-acceptance, I must get a better knowledge of who I am. I want to be kind to myself.
I put forth a lot of effort to improve my people-pleasing abilities. I'm investing my time and effort in people and places that make my heart sing. I'm gaining the ability to refuse offers from people and places that my heart aches for.

This is not a simple procedure. However, we live a more real life when we have a better grasp of who we are. This results in more satisfaction across the board.

These 5 methods can help you get a better knowledge of who you are.
1. Determine your principles and values
Knowing our principles and values is a crucial component of self-awareness.

Think about your political stance. Think about your level of religiosity. What are your opinions on some of the major problems facing the globe today? What kind of causes do you support? How do you feel about abortion, animal experimentation, and gun control laws?

These are significant concerns that will enable you to assess your moral position. They could also aid in defining your ideals.

2. Increase self-awareness
We have both internal and outward self-awareness, according to this article. The aforementioned principles and values are part of our internal self-awareness. Our ability to notice how we are regarded by others is known as external self-awareness.

Do you understand how people see you? In contrast to what you may assume, your loved ones may find you unpleasant and abrasive.
What reactions do others have to you? How well can you communicate?
Have open discussions with family and friends. Do you present the outer world with your true self?

3. Follow your instincts
Your heart no longer leaps with excitement when you get communication from someone you are consciously untangling from. Instead, there is a brief feeling of unease like a little black cloud. Trust your instincts. Don't engage in something or someone if you have a "meh" feeling about it.
Avoid attending a party if you are anxious about it. Spending half of your energy on things and people that don't make you happy will leave you fatigued and make you seem honest.

Do you appreciate who you are when you are with others or in confining circumstances? Trust your instincts. It will guide you toward a better comprehension of who you are.

4. Attend counseling.
Everybody has blind spots. We could be engaging in destructive cycles of conduct. We may have unresolved trauma from the past. Therapy is a certain technique to help us understand ourselves, no of our past.

Always keep in mind how crucial it is for you to feel at ease with your therapist. Look for a different therapist if you don't like them. Take part in and enjoy the process. You will only reap half of the rewards from therapy if you give it just half of yourself.

5. Obtain approval
Accept yourself when you reach a state of self-awareness. Accept yourself as you are and work on being content with who you are.

Avoid pushing yourself into stressful circumstances. Recognize your weaknesses and celebrate your strengths. Do more of what you find enjoyable and energizing.
Living truthfully and embracing who you are rather than attempting to live a falsehood can bring you more serenity, even if it turns out you aren't the person you thought you were.

How to Increase Self-Awareness
Meditate. Yes, do some meditation.
Your main goals and plans should be written down. Writing out your goals and monitoring your progress is one of the finest strategies to develop self-awareness.
Obtain psychometric evaluations.
Consult reliable friends.
Obtain feedback often.
Monitoring Contentment
Determine your basic belief and alter it.

The core beliefs we have about ourselves are the ones we hold the most firmly. They might be conscious or subconscious, and they have a big impact on how we see the world, think, feel, and behave. We believe these things because we have accumulated enough experience to support them. The downward arrow method may be used to identify your essential ideas. This entails tracing each idea back to the fundamental premise it was based on. Start by thinking about a concept you often hold about yourself, such as "I procrastinate too much." What does it say about me, do you think?

Your actions are influenced by your core ideas. They have deeply established views about yourself, other people, and the world around you that have been shaped by your experiences as a youngster. Core beliefs may sometimes cause cognitive distortions, which result in an incorrect perception of reality.

Deeply held convictions called core beliefs influence how individuals see the world and themselves. They significantly affect how individuals see and make decisions. Making Core beliefs may be advantageous, detrimental, or neutral. Core beliefs that are unhelpful or unrealistic may have a detrimental impact on a person's happiness in life generally and mental health.

However, since fundamental beliefs make up such a significant portion of a person's worldview, it could be challenging to recognize them. Changing ingrained views requires time and effort as well.
Cognitive behavioral therapy is centered on the idea of basic beliefs (CBT). According to Aaron Temkin Beck, whose cognitive theory provided the foundation for CBT, a person's fundamental beliefs influence how they engage with the outside world, how they handle stress, and how they connect with others.

What essential values exist?
Core beliefs are solid convictions that a person has held through time and consistently that shape their worldview and sense of self. These ideas serve as unspoken guidelines for how the world operates and what a person's place is in it.
These ideas often lack flexibility and are not always true, logical, or supported by facts. They also tend to be rigid. For instance, despite having friends, a person could believe they are essentially unlikable.
A person's ideas about other people, such as whether they think people are mostly good or evil, are also considered core beliefs.
One might have fundamental ideas that are at odds with one another. When a person's behaviors do not match their beliefs or when they have two contradicting views, this may lead to cognitive dissonance.

Core principles as examples
A core belief is any deeply held conviction that is essential to how a person interacts with the outside world or perceives themselves. Positive, negative, or neutral are all acceptable core beliefs. Here are a few instances:

Beliefs on goodness: a person's opinion of their goodness or the general kindness of others.
Beliefs such as "I am likable" and "I am likable" are examples of likability beliefs.
Worldviews: notions that include "The world is a hazardous place" and "The world is essentially unjust."
Beliefs in one's abilities, such as "I am brilliant and resourceful" and "If I work hard, I will succeed."

Where do fundamental beliefs originate?
A person's fundamental ideas evolve in reaction to their experiences. Early childhood is when they start to grow, and they keep doing so throughout time. Youngster tries to make sense of what is going on around them as they become older or to them. They form a set of beliefs as a result of their attempts to find meaning or learn from this.

However, since they originate so early, basic beliefs are not always supported by unbiased or accurate information. Unknowingly absorbing messages from family, friends, instructors, and the media may have a beneficial or detrimental impact on a person's worldview.

DO YOUR INTERNAL AFFILIATIONS—POSITIVE OR NEGATIVE—IMPACT HOW YOU SEE YOURSELF?
You automatically evaluate, assess, feel, and deduce the meaning of things as you experience life. You learn to survive by doing it. Your inner monologue is probably encouraging if, as a youngster, your family supported and validated your curiosity and healthy risk-taking. If your basic beliefs are optimistic, you will only remember life events that are consistent with your current, fact-based experiences and positive perceptions of both yourself and the outside world.

Your inner monologue will be negative if you had a dysfunctional upbringing and it will mirror your beliefs about the world and yourself. Some of the norms that individuals establish via their fundamental beliefs end up being a significant cause of anxiety and despair. One of three categories best describes negative basic ideas you have about yourself:

Helplessness
Unlovability
Worthlessness
Negative core beliefs include, for example:

There are dangers everywhere.
I am undeserving.
My bad.
I must be flawless to avoid rejection.
To avoid rejection, I must be able to read people's thoughts and offer them what they want.
Nobody wants to hear about my emotions.
Nobody wants to give you anything, so don't ask for anything.
Do not place unreasonable expectations in life.
Have you ever imagined or heard yourself utter anything similar to the words above? You could have unfavorable basic beliefs, at least about yourself. It is normal to ignore data that contradicts your main ideas and focus exclusively on that which does. The phrase "confirmation bias" refers to this idea. And that's why it might be difficult to change your fundamental ideas. Your default setting is to think in these erroneous ways. It takes time and effort to retrain your mind to think in a new way.

CORE BELIEFS ARE IMPORTANT TO ADDICTION
It is possible for unhealthy relationships and behaviors, such as drug and alcohol misuse, to be fueled by dysfunctional fundamental ideas about oneself. "I am terrible" is an illustration of a typical core concept held by addicted individuals. Carrying this responsibility is difficult. When you believe that every setback you have is something you caused, it may cause melancholy, powerlessness, poor self-esteem, and self-hatred.

To stop negative self-talk and dull their emotions, some people resort to drug misuse, food disorders, and other undesirable coping mechanisms. The detrimental basic ideas that "I am evil" or "I am unworthy" may be further fueled by addiction. The general public still has a negative view of addiction and doesn't recognize it as a sickness. Having that message reflected on you and believing that you can't quit misusing alcohol or drugs on your own will only serve to reinforce your limiting basic beliefs.

YOU CAN IDENTIFY AND DISPROVE ESSENTIAL BELIEFS.
Though it is difficult, it is extremely feasible to alter your fundamental ideas. Research has shown that cognitive behavioral therapy (CBT) is an effective method for treating trauma, mental health illnesses, and drug use disorders. The work done in CBT may be complemented by medication and other therapy.

You may confront negative core beliefs using cognitive behavioral therapy and replace them with constructive core beliefs. If CBT is a component of your drug addiction treatment, you might:

1. Recognize the circumstances, connections, or factors that are upsetting you. For instance, you could be abusing alcohol and have just ended a toxic relationship.

2. List the ideas, assumptions, feelings, and actions that are connected to the suffering. Your therapist will prod you to discuss the circumstance and pay attention to the unfavorable thoughts, feelings, and beliefs you have about yourself and the other participants. For instance, your gut and jaw may tense while you discuss your ex-partner. You could feel powerless. You can believe that you are terrible and unlovable and that you are thus not deserving of any better. You could believe that you'll never have another (satisfying) relationship. You may use alcohol as a kind of self-medication because of this.

3. Disprove false assumptions. You may question the truth of your views with the aid of your therapist. You will investigate the supporting data for your ideas. You could talk about what makes you feel worthless or awful, for instance. You'll discuss the facts that back up your claim that you don't deserve a decent relationship and that you'll never have one.

A few instances of cognitive distortions are as follows:
Extreme thinking or thinking in black and white. Nearly everything is either nice or awful. There isn't a middle ground.
Catastrophizing is expecting the worst at all times. In your imagination, a little discomfort may quickly turn into a major catastrophe.
Mental sifting: Suppressing the pleasant elements of life in favor of just focusing on the bad
Overgeneralization is when something bad happens and is applied to all situations.
Personalization is the act of assuming responsibility for circumstances that have nothing to do with you.
Knowing what others are thinking and feeling with certainty is known as mind-reading.

4. Practice using different modes of thought. Your therapist will work with you to replace unhelpful or false ideas and thoughts with constructive ones that are supported by facts. You'll discover that your basic negative ideas often lead your view to be skewed. You'll make a concerted effort to become aware of when your thoughts veer toward unfavorable fundamental beliefs, confront them, and swap them out with more truthful, powerful ones.
Positive change often occurs more quickly with cognitive behavioral therapy than with other methods. In 12 to 20 weeks of 30- or 60-minute sessions, many individuals see noticeable improvement. A novel kind of CBT called intense cognitive behavioral therapy has just been developed (I-CBT). This method calls for longer, more intense sessions spread out throughout a weekend, week, month, or even a single day. The usefulness of I-CBT is not well studied.

Get assistance in recognizing and overcoming your core negative beliefs. Negative fundamental beliefs are hard to alter, but with effort and commitment, you can modify your ways of thinking, believing, and acting such that they are healthier, more truthful, and more powerful. One of the root causes of drug and alcohol misuse is distorted basic beliefs.
In addition to a wide range of other treatments that have been shown to benefit persons battling addiction and co-occurring mental health disorders, Footprints to recovery provides cognitive behavioral therapy. To start living a healthier, more satisfying life, call us right now.

Four methods for determining basic belief.
Among the methods for determining basic beliefs are:

Observing thoughts: Pay attention to recurring ideas. These are the concepts that people often overlook. A person might begin to identify any recurring themes or patterns by increasing their awareness of them.

Keeping a journal: For a few weeks, keeping a diary to track your thoughts and emotions might be helpful. Write down the thoughts that were triggered by periods of high emotion or stress, such as after a dispute with a loved one. Review the diary after some time has passed to search for trends. For instance, a person could persistently worry about being late.

By asking questions: a person might begin to investigate the fundamental ideas that underpin their thinking after they become aware of a pattern in their thoughts. For instance, a person who worries about being late could think about what will happen, what it says about them, or why it matters whether they are late. This could enlighten them to the fact that they feel they must be flawless and that this counts because, if they are not, they will not be liked.

Take into account a person's views in the absence of proof while evaluating the evidence. Even in the face of overwhelming evidence to the contrary, if a person finds they are unable to alter their beliefs, they most likely hold core beliefs. The hardest to challenge or change thoughts frequently relates to ingrained beliefs.
People can review common core beliefs and determine which ones they hold using the worksheets or inventories that many therapists offer.

# Chapter Two

## How to identify your inner self and repair it

There are two ways to find yourself within.
Method 1: Asking the Proper Questions

1. Consider the life events that you are most proud of: Finding purpose in life is difficult, and it shouldn't be, but you may learn a lot from your history. Consider the experiences that made you feel most proud of yourself since these are often the times when you gained the greatest fulfillment and significance from your career, travels, or education.
Why are these times so unique?
What about the job surprised or enthralled you? What gave you the drive to succeed?

2. Recognize your values: Recognizing your values is a crucial step in discovering your inner self. Consider what your proudest moments teach you about your values as you consider them. Consider asking this question, "What values are connected with the things that make me proud?"
For instance, you might value education if you felt proud when you graduated from high school. You may value professional achievement if receiving a promotion at work made you feel proud. If organizing a surprise party for your mother made you feel good, you might value your family and helping others.
List all of your values as you begin. You may even organize them based on how important you think they are to you.
Knowing your values will help you choose how to live your life following them. For instance, if honesty and authenticity are among your core values, you should strive to live up to them in everything you do.

3. Identify the goals you have for your life: Looking forward as well as backward is an important part of discovering your inner self. Your desires reveal a lot about you, whether they are for a job, a house in your preferred town, a

passionate partner, or lazy Sundays with a book. Simply make a list of your life goals. Do not hold back and do not apply any filters to this list. Which are you aiming for? Which ones have you overlooked? Which is more important? When you look at your wish list and priority list, what sort of person come to mind?

4. Consider what you would do with your time if you had complete freedom: Write the book you've been wanting to, or start building a patio? Would you rather see the world or stay home and watch a movie? Would you choose the non-profit job you've always wanted or continue with an old passion if money were no object? These concepts represent a stress-free version of you; they are not simply idle dreams. Making that version of yourself a reality begins with finding her.
Think specifically and picture a complete day in the life of your desires. Sometimes it's difficult to realize these aspirations, but that's good. The key is to be aware of your aspirations and objectives since they speak volumes about your priorities.

5. Examine the knowledge, opinions, and perspectives you were raised with or took for granted: For instance, you could have hated pickles as a child but subsequently discover that they aren't all that horrible. You often tell yourself untrue things about yourself, such as "I detest pickles," "I am a morning person," or "I am brilliant at math but lousy at English," when all that is necessary is a thought. When you're very certain of anything about yourself, turn the concept around before you believe it. Do you hold this belief because it is true or just out of habit?
By adamantly declaring, "I am ________," you run the danger of overlooking those changes inside yourself.
These concepts are usually self-fulfilling. Any date you go on will make you uncomfortable and self-conscious if you constantly convince yourself that you are awkward on dates. Naturally, this makes you feel more uneasy.

6. Look through the limited categorizations that others have given you: You might be a daughter, a girlfriend, a worker, and a tennis player all at once. These labels are crucial for defining your obligations and functions in the world, but they do not constitute who you are. They are only labels, and there is much

more to you than a few words can convey. Instead, focus on the ideas that underlie these classifications.

If you identify as a daughter, consider why this position is significant to you. Is your family your life's most important foundation? Do you often resort to your family members when you're stressed?
If you consider yourself to be a girlfriend, consider what your partner brings out or emphasizes about you. Though romance does not determine who you are, developing a close relationship with someone might teach you things about yourself.

If you consider yourself an employee, consider how your objectives or viewpoints align with those of your employer. You are more than simply an employee, thus it's acceptable if they don't line up exactly.
Ask yourself what objectives you have on the court if you consider yourself a tennis player. Why do you like the sport?

7. As a starting point, take a comprehensive personality test: Personality assessments, such as the psychologically-based Meyers-Briggs test, are excellent venues for asking oneself thoughtful, insightful questions. They also provide vague, but typically helpful, ideas on how you should approach relationships, creativity, stress, and emotions. They do not, however, accurately reflect your personality. The crucial thing to keep in mind is that they are launching points for learning rather than the destination.

Which portions of the exam findings seem accurate to you after receiving them? What aspects shock you? The most crucial question is: What seems wrong or untrue, and why?
Many of these tests are available online at no cost. If you decide to, give tests with a high number of questions—at least thirty or more—a lower priority when comparing the outcomes of a few tests to reduce errors.

8. Meditate or take 10 minutes a day to ponder quietly: If you don't search for your inner self, you won't discover it. Even a few minutes of quiet sitting in a room is a terrific way to tune into oneself, so meditation is not as complicated or tough as people make it out to be. Remember that meditation is a tool to help

you think through challenging issues that you would not otherwise find the time to address.

Focus on your breathing if you're having trouble relaxing. Where does it originate? How does your body respond as you breathe in and out? What rhythm do you naturally have?

It's acceptable if your mind is racing or you feel bored. Asking yourself why you're feeling this way will stop you from feeling like you've failed in some way. What is occupying your thoughts so much in your life?

9. Keep in mind that this is a lifelong process rather than a short-term objective. Because you are always evolving, understanding who you are on the inside is a never-ending journey. You should always be searching within to learn more about yourself, as opposed to seeing your inner self as something you discover once and know forever. You change as your life and your environment do. If you think you know all there is to know about yourself, don't shut yourself up to these fresh insights.

Consider how often you were mistaken about yourself when you look back on your life. How often did your preferences, aspirations, etc., alter as you age? Even though you are confident in who you are right now, you will change as you go through life.

Method 2: Maintaining Integrity with Your Inner Self

1. Continually check in with oneself. A wonderful method to keep aware of your thoughts and emotions is to check in with yourself to see how you are feeling. One time each day, try to check in with yourself. By asking yourself questions and providing answers, you may do this by following a straightforward routine. [10]

What's the issue? You may respond, "I am anxious about my money for this month since I had to make an expensive automobile repair," in response to this.

What can I do to improve my attitude about the circumstance? You may say, "If I need to, I can make use of the emergency credit card. If I can cut down on some other areas of sending, I may be able to survive without it. It's acceptable that I spent money on this since it was a required fix."

What in my life is doing well? You may reply something like, "I have a great house, wonderful friends, and fun work," in response to this question.

2. Track goal progress and constantly reassess your objectives. Successful people and content don't merely lay out a course and pursue it without question. Your objectives need care and attention as you develop, just as your inner self does. The following questions should be asked oneself every month or so.
Are my objectives and ambitions still the same? Exist any fresh ones?
What have I done to go toward my objectives? How can I duplicate that achievement?
What can I do to actively work toward my objectives during the next two weeks?

3. Lessen how much you trust your inner critic. Daily anxieties, critiques, and self-doubt affect a lot of individuals. This is normal, but it doesn't mean you have to take their advice all the time. Remember that this is not who you are when your brain tells you something is too difficult, that you could fail, that you're not popular, or any other stressor. These are merely fears and issues that you need to deal with; your inner self is not a critic.
Ask yourself what negative thinking is being driven by an emotion—usually anger or fear. Then, rather than allowing your thoughts to spiral around in your head, you may face these feelings.
Set a timer for five minutes and listen to this voice if you're having trouble getting beyond it. Once the countdown goes off, allow yourself to feel anxious, terrified, or bewildered before continuing.

4. Assemble a group of self-aware individuals around you. Finding others who are as interested in becoming their best selves as you are can help you be yours. Good friends make everything simpler. Avoid persons who are always negative or who refuse to examine their actions. Instead, seek out others who: Are working toward their objectives.
Discuss yourself and your emotions openly.
Consider the positive side of things and look for solutions rather than justifications.

5. Develop the ability to refuse. Saying no may be challenging but is vital if you want to discover your inner self, particularly when it comes to friends, family, and colleagues. This is only a reminder to have confidence in your thoughts and choices, and not to be selfish. Trust yourself and reject the offer if it doesn't fit with your sense of who you are.

It takes some sacrifice to pursue a goal, whether it be personal or professional. But as you begin to discover your inner self, you can only decide what is vital and what is less significant.

Sometimes peer pressure is subtle and ruthless. For instance, it could be entertaining to go out with your housemates rather than complete your job or unwind. However, it's alright to momentarily disappoint them if you want or need to remain inside since they'll understand.

6. Recognize and welcome sporadic inconsistencies. The classic quote from Ralph Waldo Emerson goes, "A stupid constancy is the hobgoblin of tiny minds." He is saying that those who are genuinely self-aware recognize that their thoughts and attitudes may change and that's alright. Don't be concerned about coming off as hypocritical; the idea is to be sincere and true with yourself in the here and now, not with yourself in the past or the year before.

7. Engage in everyday challenges. It's not meant to be simple to be loyal to who you are within. You may get out of a rut and improve your talents by pushing yourself to accomplish ambitious objectives, finish tasks, or just try something new. Even better, since they force you to discover or reveal new facets of yourself, challenging yourself may frequently lead to the most satisfying experiences.

This doesn't imply that you have to have a challenging life to understand who you are. It simply implies that you don't avoid tough things because you love them or desire them.

8. Research is important, but go with your intuition. Some folks like considering every consequence before taking any action. Others will act rashly and without thinking things through. However, a sound and effective philosophy lie somewhere between these two extremes. When more research no longer helps you make a decision, it's time to take stock of your options.

9. Regularly expose oneself to new concepts, people, and activities. When you are in an unusual setting, such as a foreign nation or a gathering of strangers, you lose the context and labels that are used to describe who you are. You are free to be who you are, and these new experiences will bring out aspects of you that previously weren't necessary to reveal.

Every day, even the little thing, learn something new. You obtain a larger framework in which to evaluate yourself by expanding your grasp of the environment you live in.

10. Consult with reliable mentors or role models for advice and direction. Paradoxically, discovering your inner self is not a solo endeavor. Your self-understanding may be shaped by how other people assist you to see aspects of yourself that are hard to notice on your own. A good mentor would assist you in finding the solutions on your own rather than telling you what to do or who to be.

A mentor or role model is just someone you can confide in and with whom you can communicate freely and honestly.
A mentor is not someone who is always correct. Keep in mind that the decision to take or ignore advice is ultimately yours when asking for it.

10 Regular Exercises to Rebuild Your Self-Worth

"It took years of psychological and emotional self-destruction for you to degrade and lose confidence in yourself. Building oneself up will take days and months. Make it a practice to go within each day, connect with your emotions, and enable your spiritual side to blossom. The virtues of Vishnu

Your feelings of hatred, bitterness, and hostility are probably present as a result of a lengthy relationship and painful separation.
If you're anything like me, when all those emotions pass, you'll have a crushing sense of emptiness, loneliness, and melancholy. For a limited amount of time, alcohol and rebound romances may mask the agony. Roseanne and ice cream both only last for 26 minutes at a time.

Self Worth

Even if you just ever fought with your ex, you will suddenly find yourself in a terrible situation without them in it.
You were at least aware of your position in the world with your ex. You were aware of your purpose for being there and were adept at playing a pair. With a spouse, navigating daily life was a lot simpler. Knowing that someone was waiting for you at home, prepared to binge-watch "The Crown," gave you a sense of security, warmth, and calm.
Your life has been shattered by separation and divorce. You experience a downward cycle from rage to loneliness, humiliation to inadequacy emotions.

Increasing Your Value
You experience the agony of loss as well as the loud sound of rejection. You're overcome with a feeling of emptiness and loneliness. Who do you think you are good enough for if not your ex? You should begin focusing on your self-worth and completeness at this crucial moment. Your purpose in life is to grow into your greatest potential.

10 Regular Exercises to Rebuild Your Self-Worth
The following ten daily habits can help you regain your sense of acceptance and value.

1. Take the crutches off.
Hard drinks and revolving door romances are simply short-term fixes. You must give up the crutches that hold you back from discovering and knowing who you are and moving toward completeness.

2. Give up your grip.
Because it doesn't want to experience suffering, your mind tries to cling. You still don't want to split up, even if you were in the worst relationship imaginable or married someone similar to a "Jersey Shore" character.
No matter how much you hate each other and how damaged your relationship is, you still want to go out and have a good time with your ex in Seaside Heights.

By being conscious of the clutching, you may let it go. You realize that it has nothing to do with your ex and is instead caused by your dread of being by yourself.

With your ex, you're OK. Even if you don't like being by yourself, it doesn't improve your sense of value.

3. Permit these emotions to overtake you.

Hold the merlot in your hand and let your emotions flow over you like water. Rather than drinking more, try experiencing your sensations more. Don't restrain your feelings. Get rid of the individuals and practices that prohibit you from visiting the dark area and feeling uncomfortable.

4. Define these emotions.

Labeling emotions and being conscious of them is beneficial. Welcome your emotions like old friends and companions whenever they appear. Allow them to easily integrate into your life. Recognize that the emotions are there to support, soothe, and direct you.

Your emotions won't intimidate or terrify you anymore.

5. Get in touch with your spiritual part.

For spirituality and to reclaim your sense of worth, you don't need to go to Nepal or Bhutan on a 60-day silent retreat. Walking the dogs might be considered spiritual. The spirituality could be grinning. An act of spirituality might be recognizing another person's humanity.

What is that sober activity that uplifts your spirit and gives you the feeling of floating on a cloud?

6. Experience kindness, love, and wholeness on a deep level.

To feel whole, you could turn to religion and God. To experience love, you might look at nature and the singing of the birds. Know that you already own whatever it is that you're looking for. You need to change the way you talk to yourself, control your emotions, and be gentler to yourself. You need to establish a haven inside of your body and mind where you may reaffirm your value to yourself and treat yourself with love and care.

7. Make it a practice to visit this inner area every day.
Daily routines are crucial to developing self-love, acceptance, and value. This shift does not occur once in a lifetime. You don't suddenly start feeling better. It took years of psychological and emotional self-destruction for you to degrade and lose confidence in yourself. Building oneself up will take days and months. Make it a routine to check in with yourself, experience your emotions, and allow your spiritual side to shine.

8. Practice inner love and make affirmations to help you feel sufficient.
A thankfulness practice might help you feel better about yourself. A habit of giving and service might help you feel better. For inner healing, you may turn to nature and spirituality.

Simple verbal or written affirmations may also be helpful. Every day, your mind tries to defeat you. Go the other way. Write in a diary and use words to improve yourself. Affirmations may help you remember how valuable and whole you are.

9. Recognize your place in the larger picture.
Even though you could feel isolated and alone by yourself, you are a part of the wider cosmos. Even if you are aware that this is the case, you often forget.

When you are the foundation of everything, how can you be alone?
You wouldn't be distinct from the blouse if you were a button on a shirt. You are involved in it. You would never question your value again if you realized how linked and necessary you are. The cosmos is on your side, so you'll never feel alone again.

10. Remind yourself of all the things for which you are thankful.
You must alter your perspective and frame of mind to overcome loneliness and guilt. Turn the ideas that predominate in your head away from emotions of loneliness and inadequacy.

A thankfulness practice may change your life in this situation.
You will have less time to fret about what is absent if you can recognize what is working in
your favor and what is sufficient about you. We often devote much of our attention to what is wrong rather than what is good.


Instead of what is working in your favor, you are seeking out the opposite.
Search for the completeness, originality, and richness of your life, and you will keep discovering it.
Find out what's working in your life and what makes you feel whole by being focused and attentive about it.

# Chapter Three

## Understanding Your Emotions and Feelings

7 steps to understanding your Emotions and feelings

Step 1: The Role Emotions Play
Step 2: Don't Judge Your Emotions
Step 3: What Each and Every Emotion Feels Like & What They Convey to You
Step 4: Record Your Thoughts and Emotions
Step 5: Expand Your Emotional Vocabulary
Step 6: Share Your Emotions
Step 7: See a Therapist
Let's get to it!

Step 1: The Role Emotions Play
Emotional awareness is key to identifing your feelings & emotions
Emotional awareness is the ability to discover and understand your feelings and emotions. One of the most important determinants of how you relate to yourself and others is your level of emotional awareness. It has effect in every part of your life, starting from how you feel, the choices you always make, and what you do to manage your stress.

Emotionally intelligent individuals are more able to listen to and comprehend the emotions of others (this is empathizing). Because they are familiar with the sensation of being honest about their emotions, they are also more at ease in intimate situations.
The self-image of those who are more in touch with their thoughts and emotions is also healthier, and they are less prone to experience emotional distress when something goes wrong.
You can choose the optimal course of action by being able to recognize your feelings at any given moment. If nothing is done, you still have the opportunity to chose to take action, but at least you will be more aware of your possibilities.

Accurately understanding your emotions also helps in separating the significant from the unimportant. You learn to rely on your gut feeling and pay attention to how you're feeling within.

Don't judge your emotions at step two.
Learning to accept your thoughts and emotions without passing judgment on them is the first step to understanding them.

Accepting your sentiments requires you to refrain from criticizing others. Since many of us have been taught that it's inappropriate to experience certain emotions, like anger or grief, this may be challenging.
But every feeling has a purpose and is significant. For instance, crying is a healthy method to release tension and let go of pent-up emotions. Additionally, weeping produces neurotransmitters (such as oxytocin & endorphins) that will assist in bringing you back to happier feelings.
Being emotionally aware simply entails noticing, accepting, and processing your emotions as they come up rather than obsessing on them, talking about them constantly, or even acting on them.

Unspoken or misunderstood emotions have a long history of wreaking havoc. In addition to health issues including heart disease, sleeplessness, migraines, and digestive difficulties, they may cause worry and anxiety. Complicated sorrow, which is considerably more painful and challenging to handle than the first agony, may result from unresolved grieving.

When we suppress our feelings, they become detached from us and uncontrollable. We may better recognize them and control our conduct by bringing them into awareness.
Try to let go of your judgements about your emotions and embrace them as a natural aspect of being a person. Only after that can you start to educate yourself on how to handle them healthfully.

Step 3: How Each Emotion Feels & What It Communicates to You
By naming them, you can better understand your emotions and sensations. Sometimes it might be difficult to put words to how you're feeling. If you're feeling overpowered by intense emotions like sorrow or despair, this can happen.

In this situation, it's beneficial to pay attention to your body's responses and your thoughts. You may start to pinpoint the emotion that is producing these emotions by giving them names. The following query may be useful:

What is my body trying to tell me? Pay attention to what your body is doing if you're feeling overwhelmed and unsure of how you feel: Do you have stiff shoulders? Do you feel any tension in your stomach? Without even being aware of it, are you clenching your fists or jaw?

What emotions does my mind think I'm feeling? You could think things like, "This scenario isn't fair," or "I feel like something horrible is going to happen." Consider these concepts carefully to see if they may assist you in figuring out how you're feeling.

Then, consider what your emotions are attempting to tell you. If you take the time to discover what it is, every feeling has something to say to you. Take a step back when you have an emotion or sensation to attempt to comprehend what it implies.

Additionally, it is possible to feel many emotions at once.

For instance, you might experience guilt and embarrassment, or anger and hurt at the same time. When this occurs, make an effort to address each emotion on its own. It's simpler to use the suitable coping mechanisms that will lessen the bad impacts of your sentiments when you are aware of how you are feeling.

The Anger Voice

Anger may lead to bodily responses like feeling heated and breathing more quickly.

When you're angry, you could notice that your respiration, heartbeat, and level of shaking are all higher than normal. Your hands could tighten, and your cheeks and neck might feel warm. It's typical for us to want to shout, toss objects, and even strike out at the other person when we're furious.

You could have thoughts like "I despise him," "I can't believe she did that," "This is crazy," or "This isn't fair!" You might also feel strongly better, always eager to blame other people for your challenges, have trouble focusing, and/or consider taking vengeance.

Anger may alert us to problems that need our attention. Anger may also be a symptom that something is unjust. For instance, if you have the greatest stats in the office but are passed over for a promotion at work, you can feel upset.

You may need to establish clear boundaries or figure out healthy methods to let your anger out without harming others or yourself.
You may need to establish clear boundaries or figure out healthy strategies to deal with your rage, including learning to say "no" or taking a moment to collect yourself. Learn more about blaming, shaming, and dominating words if you suffer with rage. Even when you feel like your anger is getting the better of you, do your best to communicate in a healthy manner. If we allow anger to inspire us to improve our circumstances or habits, it may be a beneficial thing.

The Sadness Voice
Understanding emotions and feelings include unpleasant emotions like sorrow. Weakness in the heart and chest, crying, and a stronger desire to isolate ourselves from others are all symptoms of sadness. We may feel tired and find it difficult to focus on anything outside our suffering when we are sad.
People who are sad or grieving often have severe emotions of emptiness or despair, thoughts like "I'm all alone" or "this agony will never go away," the want to retreat, sleep, or weep, trouble focusing, and/or ideas about wanting to escape life.
Sadness is a sensation that may be brought on by a variety of situations, including losing a loved one, losing a job, or even ending a relationship. Sadness is a common indicator that something in our life is missing, a loss has happened, or we have been let down. Sadness indicates a desire for consolation and assistance. It could imply that we should look for ourselves and give our bodies time to mend.

The terrifying voice
The voice of terror might make you sweat, breathe quickly, and experience hyperventilation.
When you're terrified, your breathing may become shallow or you may hyperventilate. Your heart may also beat quickly and forcefully. You could even start to tremble all over or become stiff all over your body. You could feel anxious or as if something terrible is about to happen.

Your body will get ready to fight or run away if you encounter a danger. It's typical for us to feel tense and have problems focusing or thinking properly when we are terrified. Get me out of here! or "I'm about to pass out" can cross your mind. I want to flee!

One of our most fundamental and primordial emotions as humans is fear. An emotional reaction to a perceived threat of pain, danger, or injury is fear. It is typically a survival instinct to assist someone escape a harmful circumstance or at the very least be aware of the possible danger around when they experience fear.

Fear commands you to flee! While anxiety is a mood that is often brought on by the prospect of something unpleasant occurring in the future, fear is a reaction to a danger that is already present. Even when there is simply a perceived danger, anxiety nonetheless often occurs. Anxiety could be a sign that it's time to take back some of the power over your feelings or circumstances. It could also imply that you need to let go of matters beyond your control.

The Surprised Voice
When you're astonished, your heart beats quickly, and you could feel alert, lightheaded, and dizzy.
When you're astonished, your heart beats quickly, and you could feel alert, lightheaded, and dizzy. Your body might feel as if it is being jolted with electricity. You can experience overwhelm or being stuck in place. "I don't know what to do" or "I don't know how to respond" can cross your mind.

The emotion of surprise may be brought on by startling or unexpected occurrences or encounters. Being taken off guard is often the basis of feeling shocked.
It may also have its roots in the experience of having something neutral or uplifting come your way unexpectedly, like a praise or a promotion at work. When something unexpected happens, surprise signals that you need to take a moment to digest what has occurred.

The Voice Of Abhorrence

Your heart may beat more quickly or more slowly than normal, and you could feel uncomfortable or nauseous.

Your heart could beat more quickly or more slowly than normal when you're disgusted. You could feel queasy, sick to your stomach, or like throwing up. You could be thinking, "How could someone do that?," or "That's so filthy." Something that is deemed unpleasant, rude, or unethical often causes disgust. This feeling stems from the desire to stay away from poisonous items like spoiled food and dangerous chemicals. You should shove the disgusting item away from you for your protection, according to disgust.

The Voice Of Joy

Positive experiences or interactions that make you feel good often cause happiness. There may be a sense of excitement and happiness when you're satisfied. Sometimes the slightest things, like receiving a praise or completing an assignment on time, may cause delight.

Your level of happiness serves as a clue to prioritize your priorities, such as forming healthy connections with people, learning new skills, and feeling like you belong.

The Voices of Shame and Guilt.

Understanding guilt also entails understanding feelings and emotions.

Guilt is an emotion related to a personal act of misconduct. When you are feeling guilty, it feels like a severe ache in your heart, and you can feel the need to apologize to the person you offended. When you do anything that goes against your particular moral code or norms, you feel guilty. People often think, "I did something wrong," or "I should have done something different," while they are feeling guilty.

Shame, on the other hand, might make you feel as if a huge burden is resting on your shoulders, and you can feel the urge to conceal it. Shame is an unpleasant emotion that focuses on oneself. Who you are as a person is your "self." When we believe that we are flawed and imperfect as people, we experience shame. People who experience shame often think things such as, "I'm horrible," or "I'm useless."

Your sense of identity and self-esteem may suffer as a result of shame. When shame in our lives is ignored, it often leaves us feeling insecure, neglected, and alone. It is alienating loved ones and friends who could otherwise be supportive. On the other hand, guilt indicates that although what we did could have been bad, who we are as people is not. It may provide us the motivation we need to express regret and mend fences if we understand that our actions have injured someone or damaged a significant connection.

Step 4: Write Down Your Ideas and Feelings
By making a routine of journaling your emotions, you may learn to listen to and comprehend the thoughts and feelings you have.
By making it a regular habit to record your emotions each time you encounter anything new or unusual, you may learn to listen to and comprehend the feelings and emotions you go through. You'll be able to recognize your patterns and get insight into your changing feelings as a result of doing this.
What is making you to feel this way, consider it all. What is making you feel uneasy if anything? Is there a challenging assignment in your near future that might cause performance anxiety? Why are you sad if that's how you're feeling? Are you seeing a movie or television program that makes you feel that way? What may have occurred earlier today to produce the feeling?
Examine each circumstance more closely to see what is causing those emotions. Knowing your triggers can help you prevent unpleasant emotions in the future, or at the very least, learn how to deal with them more successfully.
Negative ideas often really cause the emotions we feel in reaction to them, and they may also play a significant influence in influencing emotions.
For instance: You could experience anxiety, overwhelm, and tension if you believe "I can't" or "I'll never be able to achieve this." You could feel more certain and in charge, however, if you change those ideas to something like, "This is incredibly tough, but I'm prepared to give it my best."
Determine the ideas that are closely associated with the feelings you are experiencing. Try jotting down some alternate, uplifting ideas about a circumstance and see how it affects your attitude if you wish to combat negative thinking.

Step 5: Increase Your Emotional Word Count
Expand your vocabulary to better comprehend emotions and sensations.

Expanding one's vocabulary might be beneficial for comprehending sentiments and emotions.

You may find out how you're feeling and what you need by making a list of feeling adjectives and ordering them from least to most bothersome.

If you were upset, would you describe your feelings as "a bit bothered," "irritated," "furious," or perhaps "enraged"? The word you choose may assist you in determining your place of origin and the degree of your feeling.

After that, you may make plans and take action to deal with or control your emotions. The appropriate words help you better convey your sentiments to others and offer a clearer picture of what you're going through.

Step 6: Express Your Emotions

One of the finest methods to sort feelings and emotions out is to talk about and comprehend them.

Talking about or discussing bad emotions with a trusted person is the most popular option for many individuals to let them out. It's not necessary to go into considerable detail; just speaking your troubled thoughts out can assist lessen their intensity and make it simpler to get a wider perspective.

One of the finest methods to sort feelings and emotions out is to talk about and comprehend them. When we are upset or terrified, things often look worse than they are. We may obtain insight into how to handle the issue successfully by discussing it with someone who listens without passing judgment or becoming defensive.

Step 7: Consult a counselor

It may be time to speak to someone qualified to help you healthily process your emotions if you feel that your inability to comprehend feelings and emotions is beginning to interfere with your ability to do tasks like job, study, or maintain relationships.

It may be time to speak to someone qualified to help you healthily process your emotions if you feel that your inability to comprehend feelings and emotions is beginning to interfere with your ability to do tasks like job, study, or maintain relationships.

Therapists may assist you in comprehending the interplay of certain ideas, bodily sensations, actions, and events from the past to produce emotions such as worry, shame, etc. Additionally, they may teach you techniques for "grounding" yourself when you begin to feel overburdened

# Chapter Four

## The best way to rework a tale

11 Steps To Write A New Chapter In Your Life And Change It In 2022
Fiction makes reality. They influence how we see what is and isn't conceivable, which makes it possible to do comparable behaviors and have similar consequences.
But some of the tales we tell ourselves are more harmful than helpful. and consequently must alter.

The actions listed below may help you rewrite your life's narrative and make positive changes.

1. Disarm Your Current Life Story's Negativity, Bias
3. Rewrite the Origin Story to Reshape Your Life 2. Take Responsibility for Your Creation
4. Choose a Fresh Look
5. Close out the Chapters You Don't Need
6. Eliminate the Myth of "A Concrete You"
7. Decide how to defeat your antagonist.
8. Alternate Location
9. Pick up New Talents
Improve the Supporting Cast.
11. Practice Rewriting Your Life Story to Modify Your Narrative Answers to the queries
How Can Your Trauma Story Be Rewritten?
How Should a Future Story Be Written?
Can Your Memories Be Rewritten?
Final Thoughts

Transform Your Life
1. Disprove The Pessimistic Slant in Your Present Life Story
Even though your life is balanced with both good and bad events, it is simpler to recall the bad ones.

We call this phenomenon negative bias. The first step in revising your narrative is to challenge it. Now that you are aware of your natural tendency to dwell on the unpleasant aspects of your life, you can train your mind to focus on the good aspects as well.

For instance, if you are always thinking about how you are a failure, train your mind to focus on your victories. times when you assisted someone. When you were competent.
This will assist you in being conscious of destructive thinking patterns so you can stop them before they ruin your life.

2. Claim Your Status As A Creator
When you see yourself as someone to who life continues occurring, trying to alter your tale is pointless. This indicates that you do not think you are capable of crafting the future you see. Still, you can.

It's time to assume the role of the story's author after admitting your negative bias and honing your awareness. The people involved, the setting and the desired personality are all completely up to you.

While other people's ideas may inspire you as the creator, it is ultimately up to you to choose which ones to implement. You gain self-confidence during this period, enabling you to enjoy your life as you want.

3. Rewrite Your Life's Origin Story to Improve It
Any depressing stories you are telling yourself in your thoughts need to alter since you are the author of your life story.

Examples include, "I've made Mistakes too many times." to "I've learned from my mistake and will keep trying till I succeed."
 "I was born disadvantaged but utilized those struggles to grow stronger and affect others," as opposed to "I was born disadvantaged and thus can't make an impact."
Changing your origin narrative might provide you with the motivation you need to go on. You'll likely discover the strength to improve your life when you decide to see your experiences from a different transformative viewpoint.

4. Pick A New Subject

What's the story's central theme? tragedy, disdain, endurance, love, atonement, rebirth? When you're stuck, there's a good chance that you're connecting your story to a depressing theme. But what if there was another way to see your narrative?

What if you could turn sorrow into tenacity? or from judgment to atonement. Your life feels different and your behaviors alter when your theme does.

According to research on sobering tales, drinkers who said that their most recent drinking event had improved them were more likely to remain clean and stay healthy than those who did not.

The aforementioned individuals transformed a situation that may have otherwise resulted in shame or condemnation into a tale of salvation. Changes in themes result in changes, in reality, therefore you should improve yours.

5. Cut out any unnecessary chapters

Your life is a collection of chapters, both happy and unhappy, like a book. But no, the tale doesn't have to stop after one disappointing chapter.

End a chapter when you get to it if it doesn't provide any hope for the future or if you no longer need it. No matter how challenging it is, you'll have to have the bravery to begin a new one.

A chapter's conclusion offers the opportunity to begin a new one. It sparks development, which enables you to make changes in your life.

6. Do away with the idea of "A Concrete You"

Though challenging, change is not insurmountable. But when you repeatedly attempt to change and fail, it's simple to declare, "That's simply the way I am."

But the reverse is true more than anything.

We all have our talents and flaws, but by adopting a development mindset, you may alter how you see yourself.

You can persuade yourself that you're hopelessly unmotivated, a chronic procrastinator, and unable to achieve the success you want. However, you'll find that the narrative in your head tends to shift over time as you act your way toward progress.

You must thus be aware that your behaviors are modifiable, regardless of what your present narrative may be. Every time you feel like it's all impossible, remind yourself of that.

7. Decide how to defeat your antagonist.
It's time to identify and figure out how to fight your toughest opponent now that you know you can alter any behavior you have.

What prevents you? What challenge in your life keeps coming up?

It's possible that you won't be able to defeat your foe permanently. However, you can always come up with methods to get around them.
Imagine you have a poisonous buddy that always steers you in the wrong direction. You may sever connections and get rid of them permanently. However, it's likely that something else—like the dread of the unknown—will come up, and you'll need to come up with strategies to get through it as well.

8. Alternate Location
According to research by the American Psychological Association, those who work overseas develop their creative abilities more than those who remain in their own countries. This demonstrates how shifting locales affect our tales. However, this does not imply that you must fly halfway across the globe to start again. You may alter your area, job, and favorite hangouts, among other things.

For instance, if you were accustomed to going out partying every Friday, you may choose to go camping or watch a documentary as a mental refresher.

9. Pick up New Talents
Your current life narrative is heavily influenced by the talents you have so far acquired. Your story alters once you learn a new skill.

You should thus create your tale with new abilities after changing your life in the manner described above. For instance, you may enroll in a business administration degree if you're a financial director seeking to launch a company so you can quit your 9-to-5 job and pursue financial independence.

Your career does not have to be related to your new skills. They could relate to your interests or hobbies. You would alter the course of your life as long as you are constantly learning new things.

10. Choose A More Solid Supporting Cast
It becomes inevitable that your supporting cast will change as you try to rewrite your story. You need to surround yourself with individuals that have a good impact on your life right now.
So you may associate with peers in the same profession if you're rewriting your narrative by changing occupations. You must avoid spending time with friends that encourage you to relapse any timef you want to overcome your addiction and so on.
Whatever method you use to rewrite your life's narrative, be sure to surround yourself with supportive friends and family.

11. Using practice, alter your narrative
Practice is the best method to become the person you want to be. Rewriting your tale quotations may give you the motivation to begin started, but the practice is what turns the life-altering wheel.
However, practicing might get dull, particularly once you have completed the learning curve. When it becomes habitual, it is unattractive. But of all these measures, it's the most crucial.

Consider this: You don't get healthy after only one meal on Thursday, do you? You need to eat well often.
If you want to learn graphic design, you can't wait until you feel creative; you have to put in consistent work over time.
If you wish to live a minimalist lifestyle, you cannot conceive of ever getting rid of anything. You must progressively get rid of clutter.
You see what I mean.

You can't create a reputation for what you are going to do, as Henry Ford famously stated. To put it another way, you can't keep rewriting your tale with just words.

Your tale may be revised, no matter how well-fixed you believe it to be. These actions will enable you to improve your life and eventually break free.

## Chapter Five

## Understanding Your Thoughts

Your mind is the most effective tool you have for bringing about good in your life, but if it's not used properly, it can also be the most harmful force. Controlling your thoughts entails having a say in how you live your life. Your perception and, by extension, how you interpret the world are both influenced by your mind, more specifically your thoughts. (And Here's Why Your Reality Is Based on Your Perception)

I've read that the typical human has 70,000 ideas every day. That's a lot, particularly if they are ineffective, abusive toward themselves, or simply an overall waste of energy.

You may let your mind wander, but why would you want to? Isn't it time you reclaimed control over your mind and your thoughts? Isn't it time you took the reins?

Decide to ponder your ideas intentionally and actively. Be a person who has mental control; learn to dominate your mind.

Changes to your thinking will also result in changes to your emotions, as well as the triggers that cause those sensations. You experience more mental calm as a result of both of these results.

I'm now experiencing a couple of ideas that I didn't want to have or that were a result of my reprogramming. As my mind is within my control, it is at ease right now. Yours may be as well!

Before you can take control of your ideas, you must acknowledge that you are now under the power of some unwelcome "squatters" who have taken up residence in your mind.

Knowing who they are and what drives them will allow you to rule over them and evict them if you want to be the boss of them.

Here are four of the "squatters" in your mind who produce harmful ideas.

1. The Internal Critic
This is your ongoing abuser, who frequently consists of:

The opinions of others, often your parent's
thoughts that you have formed based on your expectations or those of other
people
comparing yourself to others, particularly celebrities and public figures
the lies you tell yourself after unpleasant events like betrayal and
disappointment. Your perception gives rise to your self-doubt and self-blame,
which in situations of rejection and betrayal are probably unfair.
Pain, poor self-esteem, a lack of self-acceptance, and a lack of self-love are the
Inner Critic's driving forces.

If not, why would they harm you? Additionally, why would you abuse yourself
if this person is you? Why would you allow someone to give you a poor treat?

2. The Anxious
This individual lives in the future, in the "what if" universe.
Fear, which is frequently unreasonable and unfounded, drives the Worrier. This
individual may sometimes act out of worry that the same thing may happen
again.

3. The Troublemaker or Reactor
This one is the one that makes people angry, frustrated, and hurt. These set-offs
result from old wounds that haven't yet healed. He will get agitated by any event
that is even remotely connected to a previous injury.
This individual may be triggered by thoughts, emotions, noises, and even scents.

The Reactor lacks true motivation and exhibits erratic behavior. He is controlled
by old programming that, if it ever did, does not benefit you anymore.

4. The Sleep Deprived
This may combine any number of distinct squatters, such as the inner worrier,
inner critic, inner ruminator, inner planner, and inner rehashed.
As a response to stillness, which he struggles against, the sleep-deprived person
may be motivated by: Taking care of the business you ignored during the day

Self-doubt, a poor sense of self-worth, unease, and widespread uneasiness
For the inner critic and worrier, see the list above
How are these squatters to be controlled?


How to Control Your Thoughts
You are the one thinking and watching your ideas. You can manage your
thoughts, but you must be aware of them to recognize "who" is in charge of
them. Based on this, you may choose the strategy you should use.

Start each day to be conscious of your thoughts and recognize when you are
having negative ones.

You may regulate your thoughts in one of two ways:

Technique A: Disrupt them and change them
Technique B: completely get rid of them
Peace of mind is what is referred to as the second choice.

The interrupt-and-replace technique may be used to retrain your subconscious.
In time, the replacement concepts will replace the original ones as the "go-to"
ones in applicable situations.
Use Technique A to deal with the Inner Critic and Worrier, and Technique B to
deal with the Reactor and Sleep Depriver.

1. The Inner Critic:
When you discover yourself thinking negatively about yourself (beating
yourself up, calling yourself names, etc.), stop yourself.
You may mentally shout "Stop! No" or "Enough! I'm in charge right now. Then,
instead of whatever negative thinking you had about yourself, think something
positive or affirm anything that starts with "I am."

You may, for instance, change the idea "I'm such a loser" to "I am a Divine
Creation of the Universal Spirit." I am a wonderful spiritual entity growing in
my understanding of the human condition. I am an energy, light, and material
existence. I am amazing, wise, and lovely. I accept and adore myself just as I
am.

If you know whose voice it is, you may engage in a debate with yourself to invalidate the "voice" that generated the thought:
It's not true just because so-and-so called me a loser, you know. It was not a declaration of fact, only his or her opinion. Maybe they were kidding, but since I'm insecure, I took it seriously.

To be prepared, you might write down or plan your counterthoughts or affirmations if you notice that you often think self-critical thoughts.
You should remove this intruder first, if necessary by force:
They make the Warrior angry.
He also keeps the Reactor present because the names you call yourself turn into triggers when used by other people.
He perpetuates the Sleep Depriver because they are frequently present when you try to fall asleep.
They bully people and abuse them verbally and emotionally.
They undermine one's self-worth. They persuade you that you are not deserving. They are lying! Get them out for the sake of your self-worth!
By getting rid of your harshest critic, you will also make the other three squatters less noticeable.
Change them out with your new closest pals who will uplift, inspire, and improve your life. You want to have this presence in your head.


2. For the Anxious
Long-term anxiety is detrimental on a mental, emotional, and physical level. It can ruint your health in the long run.
Fear sets off the body's fight-or-flight reaction, worries the mind, and induces anxiety. You might find it more challenging to effectively manage your thoughts as a result.

A "worry thought" should be easy to spot by the way it makes you feel. The following physiological symptoms indicate that the fight-or-flight reaction to terror has begun:

elevated heartbeat, blood pressure, or adrenaline rush
shallow breathing or inability to breathe

tensed muscles

Any worry-related thought should be interrupted using the aforementioned technique, and then replaced. Instead of worrying, however, you'll think positively about the result you want this time.

This is the perfect moment to interact with your higher power if you believe in one. Here's an illustration:

I say the following (I refer to it as a prayer) instead of stressing out about my loved ones traveling in terrible weather:

"I appreciate you, wonderful spirit, keeping watch over. Thank you for keeping an eye on his/her automobile and ensuring that it is always safe, roadworthy, and free of maintenance difficulties. Thank you for only putting safe, responsible, and attentive drivers around him/her. And I appreciate you keeping him/her safe, responsible, and awake.

When you consider it or say it out loud, smile, and use the present tense. You may feel it and perhaps even start to believe it with the aid of both of these.

If you can see the outcome of your prayer, the visualization will strengthen your emotions and have a greater influence on your vibrational field.

Take a quiet breath right now, gently inhaling through your nose and exhaling through your mouth. Take whatever many you like! Continue doing that until you sense that you are almost in control of your thoughts.

The Reactor will lose steam if frightened thinking patterns are replaced with ones of thankfulness.

For instance, the common parental response after the first, frightening thought of discovering your kid wandering at the mall is to scold them.

"I warned you not to stray from my presence." The child's dread of becoming lost in the first place is only increased by this response.

Additionally, it teaches kids that their parents will be upset if they make a mistake, which might lead them to lie to you or withhold information from you in the future.

When you have scared thoughts, change them:

"I appreciate You (your chosen Higher Power) keeping an eye on my kid and keeping him secure. I appreciate your helping me locate him quickly.

After going through this procedure, your sole response will be appreciated when you meet your kid, which seems like a preferable option for everyone concerned.

3. Concerning the Disruptor, Reactor, or Over-Reactor
It will take a little more time and thought to find and repair the sources of the triggers to permanently remove this intruder. But until then, you may keep the Reactor under control by starting to breathe consciously as soon as you become aware of his presence.

The fight or flight reaction is triggered by the Reactor's thoughts or emotions, just as it is with the Worrier. He will exhibit the same physiological indicators of his presence. You should be able to distinguish between worry, rage, frustration, and pain with a little concentration.
You've probably heard the advice to count to 10 when you're furious; but, by deliberately breathing throughout that time, you may make considerably greater use of those ten seconds.

Being aware of your breathing is all it takes to practice mindful breathing. Pay attention to the air entering and leaving the space.
You should inhale via your nose:
As the air enters your nose, feel it.
Feel your lungs expanding and filling up.
Think about feeling your belly rise.
Through your nose, exhale:

Empty your lungs as you read.
Observe your belly tumbling.
As the air leaves your nostrils, feel it.
For as long as you like, continue this. You are free to leave the circumstance. Thus, the adrenaline has time to return to normal. You can now approach the situation with a more composed, logical perspective, refrain from acting negatively, and you'll have more control over your thoughts.

This squatter's problems include aggravating the sleep-deprived person's problems. You can prevent reactionary behavior, which will lessen the need for the rehashing and ruminating that might prevent you from falling asleep, by evicting or at the very least controlling the Reactor.

Control your thoughts to prevent the Reactor from causing stress in your life and your relationships.
Find your true motivation first and foremost. What inner motivation can keep you moving forward? Join the free Fast-Track Class - Activate Your Motivation if you're unsure. You may discover your inner drive and construct your motivational engine around it with the aid of this complimentary intense session. Join the no-cost meeting here.

4. For the sleep-deprived (composed of the inner-planner, inner-rehashing, and inner-ruminator, as well as the inner-critic and inner-worrier).
I suffered from a pretty typical issue: I couldn't shut my thoughts down at night. Because of this difficulty, I was unable to fall asleep and therefore have a comfortable and rejuvenating night's sleep.

How I conquered my mind and drove the Sleep Depriver and all of his friends out is detailed below.

I tried to block out my thoughts at first by paying attention to my breathing and the rise and fall of my belly, but it didn't work for very long. (Actually, I now begin by examining the posture of my mouth when at rest to prevent clenching.) Then I developed a substitute technique that prevented uncontrollable thinking: visualizing the word in while inhaling and the word out while exhaling. To equal the length of my breath, I would (and do) lengthen the term.
I go back to thinking in and out when I find myself doing so. With this method, my thoughts are still kind of whirling, but they are no longer uncontrollably so. I have power over my thoughts and I decide to be silent.

I began yawning after only a few cycles when I first tried this technique, and I generally fall asleep within ten minutes.
On particularly trying nights, I boost my focus by keeping my eyes in a looking-up posture (closed, of course). I sometimes attempt to stare in the direction of my third eye, but it greatly hurts my eyes.

I urge you to try this method if you have difficulties falling asleep because you can't turn off your thoughts. I continue to use it each night. Starting tonight, you can get better rest!

Additionally, you can apply this method whenever you want to:

In case you wake up too early, go back to sleep.
Put your mind to rest.
Relax your emotions
Just concentrate on the here and now.
the conclusion
Your mind is a tool that may be utilized either constructively or destructively, just like any other instrument.
you may let noxious, unpleasant, and unwelcome renters fill your thoughts, or you can pick peaceful, grateful, compassionate, loving, caring and joyful tenants.

Your mind has the potential to become your closest companion, your staunchest ally, and a reliable source of support. Your ideas are something you can control. You have a choice!